Lel

MW00988189

LEGENDARY BASKETBALL PLAYER

Written by: Jackson Wells

TABLE OF CONTENTS

Who is LeBron James?

Everyone who knows Basketball is aware of who LeBron James is but if you are not allow yourself to be surprised by this legend.

Just like how every superhero has a story about how they became a hero, famous sports players also have their own stories. One of them, named James, was born in really hard times. He and his family had a tough life while growing up because of things they couldn't control. Sadly, not everyone gets to have both their parents around when they're growing up. This was the case for

James. Not everyone gets to live in the same home for a long time, enjoying things like watching cartoons and eating yummy cereal. Not everyone goes to the same school for years and makes friends they've known for a long time, as he did.

This is why heroes are important to all of us. They show us that we can be successful and make our dreams come true even when life is really tough at the start. You don't need a lot of money to achieve your goals. Even if you think your life has been hard and your friends have more stuff than you, it doesn't mean you're worth any less. It doesn't mean you won't achieve just as much as they will. We know this is true because of LeBron James and his story of success.

Story of Birth and early childhood

On an ordinary day in Akron, Ohio, LeBron Raymond James Sr. was born on December 30, 1984. This seemingly usual event marked the start of an extraordinary journey that would see LeBron rise from modest beginnings to become a global icon in the world of sports and beyond.

LeBron's story isn't just about his achievements on the basketball court; it's a powerful narrative of resilience, determination, and the unshakable belief that no matter where you come from, you can shape your destiny.

LeBron's mother, Gloria James, was only 16 years old when she gave birth to him. His father, Anthony McClelland, wasn't present in his life due to their separation before LeBron's birth. Growing up without a father figure presented its challenges, but LeBron's early years were marked by the strength of his mother and his innate drive to carve his path forward.

Gloria's journey as a young mother was far from easy. Juggling parenthood and education demanded significant effort and sacrifice. Being a teenage parent meant facing the pressures of providing for her child while still growing up herself. Yet, Gloria's determination shone through as she completed her high school education while working various jobs, including as a retail clerk and using her accounting skills to support their needs.

Financial constraints often led Gloria to seek help from her mother, Freda, who also understood the struggles of single parenthood. This familial support played a crucial role in shaping LeBron's upbringing. It was evident that strong family bonds were the foundation upon which LeBron's future would be built.

The financial challenges Gloria faced often required frequent moves from one place to another, disrupting LeBron's stability. Changing schools and leaving behind friends created a sense of upheaval that could have easily discouraged him. However, amid these changes, a gift from Gloria ignited a passion within LeBron that would prove pivotal in shaping his destiny. At the age of three, she gave him a basketball hoop, unknowingly planting the seeds of his love for the game.

LeBron's natural talent for basketball quickly emerged. His dedication and hard work on the court set him apart. Despite the obstacles he encountered, his passion for the sport became his refuge, a place of solace amid life's uncertainties.

As LeBron matured, his basketball skills flourished, catching the attention of coaches and scouts nationwide. While his prowess on the court was evident, it was his work ethic that truly distinguished him. He showed that persistence and determination were key ingredients in the recipe for success.

However, LeBron faced setbacks and disappointments along the way. Yet, he tackled these challenges with the same determination that defined his journey. He transformed setbacks into stepping stones, using them as motivation to strive for improvement.

LeBron's journey didn't only include personal victories; he also prioritized team dynamics. His leadership and ability to uplift those around him became his hallmark. He empowered his teammates, encouraging them to aim higher and believe in their potential.

Beyond the court, LeBron's influence expanded exponentially. He became a role model, inspiring people globally to overcome obstacles through hard work, dedication, and a positive mindset. His story resonated across diverse backgrounds, motivating countless individuals to pursue their dreams against all odds.

LeBron's story illustrates the power of persistence, resilience, and the belief that any obstacle can be overcome. From a challenging upbringing to global acclaim, he shows that with unwavering dedication, hard work, and a positive mindset, anyone can transcend their circumstances and achieve greatness. LeBron's journey will continue to inspire generations, reminding us that the pursuit of dreams is worth every effort, regardless of our starting point.

With these words, we celebrate LeBron James not just as a basketball superstar but as a living testament to the triumph of the human spirit. This tale of triumph over adversity, of pushing beyond limits and defying odds, serves as a beacon of hope for all who dare to dream.

Young Lebron's Interest in Sports

When LeBron hit the age of 10, his go-to game wasn't basketball – it was American football! He had a real knack for it, managing to score a whopping 19 touchdowns in just six games. People were starting to think he could become a big football star someday.

However, the school wasn't exactly smooth sailing for LeBron. With all the moving around and a tough upbringing, his schoolwork suffered. This caught the attention of his football coach, Frank

Walker, who stepped in to help. Frank made a kind offer to LeBron's mom – he offered to let LeBron live with him so he could focus on school and sports.

During the two years LeBron spent with Frank, things started looking up. He did better in school, and he also got introduced to another sport: basketball. Even though LeBron had a basketball hoop since he was a toddler, he didn't know how to play until then. Frank showed him the ropes, and LeBron quickly got the hang of it. He had a natural talent for the game and loved playing it.

After his time with Frank, LeBron went back to live with his mom in a new place. But his passion for basketball didn't fade. He continued to get better, and his family and friends kept supporting him along the way.

In the background, LeBron's journey in basketball was taking off. He joined a team called the Shooting Stars, coached by Dru Joyce Jr. LeBron's buddies, including Little Dru, were also part of the team. They practiced at a local center and even managed

to win a big national competition.
What's even more impressive?
They won that same competition
six times in a row!

This part of LeBron's story teaches
us about adapting from one sport
to another and the value of having
people who believe in you. Frank
and LeBron's friends played a big
role in his growth, both on the
court and in life.

As we continue to follow LeBron's
journey, we'll see how he faced
and conquered challenges. His
story reminds us that with

mentors, hard work, and a whole lot of passion, we can achieve incredible things. Just like LeBron, we can overcome obstacles and reach our dreams when we're surrounded by people who care about us and when we give our all to what we love.

Sophomore Year in Highschool

Remember how LeBron was good at football back in the day? Well, he continued to play football in high school as well. During his first year of high school, LeBron played as a wide receiver in football. His role was to run quickly down the field, catch passes from his teammate who throws the ball, and score touchdowns. People recognized LeBron as a skilled catcher.

Some folks think he could have become a football star because of how good he was. However, those who supported his basketball career were concerned that he might get hurt while playing football, which could end his career. Even his mother worried about the risks and hoped he would stop.

Despite these concerns, LeBron had a fantastic season in football. He scored 15 touchdowns! He was faster than many other players, and he was amazing at catching the ball.

He continued to show that he wasn't just good at basketball, but he was also a talented athlete. His coaches believed he could even play in the NFL!

At the same time, in basketball, LeBron was doing well. In his first high school game, he scored 15 points.

His highest score in high school was 27 points! Those are the kinds of scores you usually see from the best players in the NBA.

LeBron's friends on the basketball team were also performing well. As all of this was happening, LeBron was becoming famous. He was being asked for interviews, attending press conferences, scouts were watching him play, and sports writers were interested in him. LeBron was even invited to the Five-Star Basketball Camp, which was a big deal for up-and-coming basketball talents. Famous players like Michael Jordan had been a part of it too!

During his freshman year, LeBron's high school basketball

team never lost a game. He
showed his skills both at his
school and at the Five-Star camp.

After the camp, he was chosen not
only for the all-star team but also
to play with older kids in a more
advanced division. LeBron's
reputation as a rising basketball
star was spreading across the
sports world. Recruiters wanted
him to leave his school and join
another high school team, and his
current school's basketball team
was also gaining more popularity.

In his sophomore year, LeBron's team won the championship for the second time. They did lose their first game that season to another team called Oak Hill, which had been unbeaten until they faced LeBron's team. Imagine being on a basketball team that only loses their first game in their second season! Even though they lost that game, LeBron managed to score 35 points during it. Not many NBA players can say they score that many points in a regular game. LeBron achieved this while still in high school. On average, he scored 25 points per game during the season. His efforts helped his school, St. Vincent, win another championship title, and he was named sophomore of the year by Sporting News.

Junior Year of the Legend

GOODBYE TO FOOTBALL

When LeBron reached his third year at St. Vincent's, he realized that he could no longer continue his football career due to an unusual injury - a broken finger. While this injury wasn't enough to end his career, it did bring about a significant change in LeBron's life.

Furthermore, the challenges of excelling in both football and basketball at a high level, along with the demands of school, became apparent. Even exceptional athletes like LeBron recognized their limits, and this realization marked one of his boundaries.

In the same year, another pivotal event occurred as Coach Dambrot decided to leave his coaching position to join a university team. While coaching LeBron and contributing to the team's consecutive championships was noteworthy, Dambrot likely saw the new opportunity as a career advancement.

Naturally, LeBron and his teammates were disappointed by Dambrot's departure, hoping there might be a way to retain him. Nevertheless, they had to come to terms with the fact that they would need to strive for greatness without him. Fortunately, Coach Dru stepped in to take his place, a familiar face from LeBron's Shooting Stars days.

LeBron's prominence continued to rise during his junior year, as he remained a sought-after figure for interviews, comments, and press conferences. His presence even extended to major basketball publications, notably being featured on the cover of Sports Illustrated, a prestigious American sports magazine. While it wasn't unprecedented for a high school athlete to grace the magazine's cover, it was unusual for a junior to achieve this distinction - a testament to LeBron's penchant for achieving the extraordinary.

Despite their status as basketball stars, LeBron and his teammates still faced the inevitable hardships of losses. Regardless of one's skill level, experiencing significant defeats is an unavoidable aspect of sports. In his junior year, St. Vincent experienced a loss to Oak Hill, with LeBron contributing an impressive 36 points. Regrettably, his remarkable performance couldn't secure victory for St. Vincent. However, the most challenging loss of the season came when they were defeated by Roger Bacon, bringing an end to St. Vincent's two-year championship streak. As always LeBron took the loss seriously and was willing to come back stronger.

Senior Year of Budding Player

Unfortunately, LeBron's bad luck continued after his defeat in his senior year. During the summer following his junior year, while playing in tournaments for the Shooting Stars with his friends, LeBron had a serious injury. It was so bad that he had to be taken to the hospital. He had broken his wrist and needed a cast for his arm.

LeBron had to take a break from playing for a few weeks. But by the end of the summer, he was back on his feet and ready to play basketball again. There were high hopes for his senior year to be amazing. His team was getting ready to travel around the country to play against big teams. They even arrived at a game in a fancy limousine and had one of their matches shown on TV. Their fame, along with LeBron's, kept growing. They even sold bobblehead figures of LeBron to basketball fans! Other items related to LeBron started popping up online, including basketballs claiming to have his signature. Despite all this attention, LeBron and his team lived up to the excitement. They began the season strong, winning against their opponents easily. LeBron scored his highest number of points ever at that time — 50 points. Not long after, he scored 52 points in a game against a team in Los Angeles.

Apart from excelling in his senior year, LeBron had another big decision to make: What would he do after high school? Throughout his career, LeBron had always achieved remarkable things that amazed everyone. Now that he

was finishing high school, what
could he do that would be
historic? What was the most
exceptional thing he could achieve
in his senior year at St. Vincent's?

LeBron had a few options. He had
already accomplished something
by scoring 52 points. But the most
daring thing he could do was to
jump straight from high school
basketball to playing
professionally in the NBA. This
was a difficult feat to accomplish.
One of the reasons was the
disagreement between the NBA
and college basketball (NCAA).

They were in a dispute. Imagine trying to manage a successful basketball team that wins many games. You would need great players to ensure victory. But what if you weren't sure if your players would stay with your team? What if another league kept taking away your players? That's what was happening between the NBA and NCAA. Every basketball player's dream was to play in the NBA, and the NCAA came second. So, the NCAA wanted to make sure players couldn't skip college and go straight to the NBA or leave for the NBA before completing their college education. They agreed that players had to start and finish college before moving on to the NBA.

Luckily for LeBron, this agreement between the NBA and NCAA eventually broke down. Now he could go directly from high school to the NBA. Everyone believed he was good enough. He had consistently shown that he was a future basketball star. Magazines and journalists even started calling him "the chosen one." But was he it? Only time will tell.

NBA Draft and LeBron's Future

Can a policy decide your future? It sure can, especially in sports. Let's see what this draft is and how it ended up for our player.

In the NBA, there's a rule that helps teams that didn't do well in the season. These teams get the chance to pick the best new players joining the NBA. This is to make things fair and competitive. Every team should have a shot at having the best players on their team.

This way of picking players makes sure that it's not just the richest teams that always get the best players. If that were the case, the teams with less money would always struggle in the season. They wouldn't have a chance at winning championships or beating the best teams. It would all depend on who has more money to spend.

But because of the Draft, things are different. It helps make sure that everyone has a fair chance.

One team that wasn't doing well was the Cleveland Cavaliers. They had lost many games and didn't win much. Because of how the Draft works, they got a good opportunity to choose first. That's when they made history by picking LeBron James. He had just finished high school and was chosen to play professional basketball in the NBA for the Cleveland Cavaliers, even though he had faced tough times growing up.

Welcome to NBA- First Season

The pressure was really on now.
People were wondering how well
LeBron would do, even his
teammates had doubts about if he
could handle it. They thought that
players who went straight from
high school to the NBA often
didn't meet the high expectations.
They didn't think LeBron would
be any different.

But it didn't take long for LeBron
to prove them wrong. Just six
months after finishing high school,
he was ready to start in an NBA

game against the Sacramento Kings. Imagine how nervous he must have been! So much was riding on this game. The Kings were a tough team to beat, much better than the Cavaliers, and had some NBA stars on their side.

With all eyes on him, LeBron didn't let the pressure get to him. He showed everyone how amazing he was. He scored 9 points in the first 10 minutes and ended with a total of 25, showing he was unstoppable. This surprised his critics and thrilled his fans. He showed the world that he was something special.

Even though LeBron played well, the Cavs lost the game. This made him sad; he felt like he should have done more to help the team win. This feeling wasn't new for him. Remember that championship game where he scored 36 points but his team still lost? It was the same feeling. He cared more about his team doing well than just his performance. That's what makes him great.

The Cavaliers didn't do very well after that game. They lost the next five games. Considering they had the most losses the previous season and had one of their worst seasons ever, it probably felt like history repeating itself. LeBron finally got his first NBA win when they beat the Washington Wizards, but the team was still struggling. His efforts alone weren't enough to carry the team to victory. So, what did LeBron do? He decided to play as a point guard. The point guard is like the main player who controls the ball most of the time and tells others what to do. This was a big job, especially for an 18-year-old straight out of high school. But LeBron was up for the challenge.

And true to form, LeBron was excelling as a point guard. The team started doing much better. His teammates had warmed up to him and trusted him on the court. The team that had only won 17 games the previous season was now on a 7-game winning streak!

LeBron was having the same kind of positive impact he had on his past teams, like the Shooting Stars and St. Vincent. He was also setting records left and right. In a game against the Nets, he scored 40 points. While not as high as his 52 points in high school, he became the youngest player in the NBA to score that many points in a game! Apart from that, he was consistently scoring more than 30 points per game. This was a guy who had just finished high school, scoring these numbers in the toughest basketball league in the world. LeBron was proving he was truly one of a kind.

By the end of the season, the Cleveland Cavaliers had won 35 games and lost 47. Even though they had more losses than wins, remember that before LeBron came, they had only won 17 games the previous season. Out of the remaining games, they lost 65. LeBron's presence was making a real difference. For his hard work, he won Rookie of the Month in his division every month and eventually became the Rookie of the Year. He was only the second high school player to win this award. He averaged almost 21 points per game that season.

Everyone was looking forward to this amazing youth's rise.

The Second Season- Journey Continued

By now, you probably know that LeBron James hates losing. He's all about making his team the best and racking up those wins. So, when his second season with the Cleveland Cavaliers rolled around, he had one mission: make sure they did way better than the last time.

LeBron was stepping up his game in a big way. The team was also starting to see him as a leader. In that second season, his average points per game shot up from around 21 to a whopping 27. And he wasn't just scoring – he was snagging rebounds and dishing out assists like a pro.

His performance was turning heads, and he even nailed a Triple Double. That's when a player hits double digits in points, rebounds, and assists all in one game. LeBron pulled it off with 27 points, 11 rebounds, and 11 assists against the Portland Trail Blazers. But that's not all. He also dropped a jaw-dropping 56 points against the Toronto Raptors, becoming the

youngest player to do that in an
NBA game. He even got the nod
to play in the NBA All-Star game,
where the best players of the
season get to show off their skills.

Throughout the season, the team
was picking up steam. They
managed 42 wins against 40
losses, a big improvement from
before. If you had seen the
Cavaliers struggling in the two
previous seasons, you would've
bet on them getting better – and
you'd be right.

In just two seasons, LeBron had put himself on the map as one of the NBA's heavy hitters. He was racking up individual achievements left and right. But there was still a hurdle to cross. Even though he was doing great individually, his team was still facing challenges. If he wanted to be the greatest player of all time, he had to pull off something crazy – win an NBA championship with the Cleveland Cavaliers.

The Third Season- Playoffs

By his third season in the NBA, LeBron was consistently improving and showing better performance with each game. More importantly, his team was also making progress. They finished that season with an impressive record of 50 wins and 32 losses, which was a significant improvement compared to the three seasons before!

Their strong performance earned the Cavs a spot in the NBA championship playoffs. To win the championship, they needed to

succeed in four rounds of playoffs.
In the first round, they performed
exceptionally and defeated the
Washington Wizards.
Unfortunately, their journey
ended there. They were defeated
by the Wizards in the second
round of the playoffs.

However, this setback didn't
discourage LeBron and his team.
The following season, they came
back stronger. With 50 wins under
their belt, they secured a spot in
the playoffs once again. The team
had acquired new players to
enhance their strength. They

triumphed over the Wizards in the first round, defeated the Nets in the second, and bested the Pistons in the third. This journey led them to face the San Antonio Spurs in the NBA finals. This was a huge opportunity for the Cavs to achieve their dreams. Sadly, the San Antonio Spurs proved too formidable. The Cavs lost in the finals, leading to a heart-wrenching experience for LeBron and his teammates. As was his nature, LeBron took the loss to heart and blamed himself for it.

LeBron's fourth season with the Cavaliers showcased just how much the team had evolved after their long journey. They achieved an astounding 66 wins and only suffered 16 losses that season. They had transformed from the team they were when LeBron first joined. And, as expected, LeBron himself was continually improving.

He was performing so remarkably that he was awarded the Most Valuable Player (MVP) title that season. He celebrated this achievement at St. Vincent-Mary, where it all began. He went on to win the MVP award again in his fifth season with the Cavaliers.

Despite these incredible achievements, the NBA championship remained elusive for LeBron. They hadn't returned to the finals since their loss to the Spurs. Regardless of all the hard work, LeBron put in, they couldn't do enough to secure an NBA championship.

LeBron and the Miami Heat

LeBron James was part of Team USA when he was playing Olympics. He wasn't the only one though there were three standout players on that team — LeBron, Dwayne Wade, and Chris Bosh. These three became the dream team how they work well together.

Team USA was unbeaten at the Olympics and won the finals comfortably. It was revealed that Chris Bosh would join the Miami Heat after the 2010 Olympics. LeBron debated whether to join his Miami Heat colleagues and attempt to win the title of NBA champion there as the 2011–12 season approached.

He knew that his Cleveland Cavaliers teammates and supporters would be devastated if he didn't choose them. Making a decision was challenging.

LeBron, however, went with his gut. He ultimately decided to join the Miami Heat. The Big Three — LeBron James, Dwayne Wade, and Chris Bosh — became well-known very quickly. The general impression was that these three would go far because of how well they played together.

LeBron and his teammates were
doomed to share the same curse as
the Cavaliers during their first
season together.

Despite making it to the playoffs,
they got beaten by the Mavericks.
But true to form, LeBron returned
the next season with a fresh start.
With 46 wins and 20 losses, they
had a successful season.

Again, LeBron was named MVP.
Now was the time for the
postseason. The Pacers lost to
them. After defeating the Celtics,
they prepared to take on the
Oklahoma City Thunder in the
2012 championship game. A

player making headlines on that team named Kevin Durant was LeBron's toughest rival there. But they had other weapons besides him. Russell Westbrook and James Harden were also available. LeBron would find that this was his most difficult challenge yet. The Big Three gave it their all on that day in 2012 when they faced the OKC Thunder. Last but not least, LeBron, the young Akron child who rose to NBA MVP status, captured his first NBA title.

LeBron had put all of his knowledge to use.

LeBron applied all the knowledge he had gained over the previous years to assist his team win.

He highlighted the importance of never giving up. They competed against the Spurs, who handed him his first significant defeat in the NBA Finals, the following year. But the Big Three weren't worried about it. The Miami Heat defeated the Spurs in the NBA Finals of 2013 to win the title twice.

Win for the Cavaliers

The Miami Heat's impressive streak of wins in the NBA finals ended during the 2014 NBA finals when they were defeated by the Spurs. At the end of that season, LeBron's contract was up, and he decided to return to the Cleveland Cavaliers. Armed with all the experience he had gained, he was determined to finish what he had started with the Cavs. They had a strong season and managed to secure a spot in the playoffs.

After enduring a long series of losses that seemed unending, and with hopes pinned on LeBron to turn the tide, he led the Cavaliers to victory in the finals against the Golden State Warriors. It was a dream come true for LeBron, and he had finally achieved what he had set out to do. Following this achievement, he went on to play for the Lakers, the team he is still a part of today.

CONCLUSION

LeBron James is surely the sporting hero of many with his many wins and even more resilience he is exemplary.

He demonstrated how to take good decisions with your mind and not just your heart by choosing basketball over football or its teams.

It takes courage to take decisions for yourself and what you believe in. That's the main lesson of his life, you have a future in your hand, and it' certain that you will get what you have been fighting for.

ACHIEVEMENTS AT A GLANCE

These are not all the achievements but some highlights of LeBron's career

- 4 times NBA champion (2012, 2013, 2016, 2020)
- 4 times NBA Finals MVP (2012, 2013, 2016, 2020)
- 4 times NBA Most Valuable Player (2009, 2010, 2012, 2013)
- 19 times All-Star (2005–2023)
- 3 times NBA All-Star Game MVP (2006, 2008, 2018)

- NBA All-Defensive Second Team (2014)
- NBA Rookie of the Year (2004)
- NBA All-Rookie First Team (2004)
- NBA scoring champion (2008)
- NBA assists leader (2020)
- NBA 75th Anniversary Team
- AP Athlete of the Decade (2010s)
- 4 times AP Athlete of the Year (2013, 2016, 2018, 2020)

QUOTES BY LEBRON JAMES

Following are some note-worthy advice and comments by LeBron, enjoy.

- *There is a lot of pressure put on me, but I don't put a lot of pressure on myself. I feel if I play my game, it will take care of itself.*

- *I have short goals - to get better every day, to help my teammates every day - but my only ultimate goal is to win an NBA championship. It's all that matters. I dream about it. I dream about it all the time, how it would look, how it would feel. It would be so amazing.*

- *I played football for a team called the East Dragons on the east side of town. We only had six regular-season games. And six games I played tail back and I had 18 touchdowns in six games. That's when I knew I had some athletic ability.*

- *I never get too high on my stardom or what I can do.*

- *As a professional athlete a lot is going to be said about you - but I just try to move forward and try to achieve my goals.*
- *"I'm going to use all my tools, my God-given ability, and make the best life I can with it.*

- *You know, my family and friends have never been yes-men: 'Yes, you're doing the right thing, you're always right.' No, they tell me when I'm wrong, and that's why I've been able to stay who I am and stay humble.*

    "

- *I always say, the decisions I make, I live with them. There are always ways you can correct them or ways you can do them better. At the end of the day, I live with them.*

REFERENCES

Gurnett, B. (2018). LeBron James: Making the Case for Greatest of All Time. Sterling Children's Books.

Lew Freedman. (2008). LeBron James: A Biography. Greenwood Press

https://www.inc.com/marcel-schwantes/10-lebron-james-quotes-from-his-legendary-career-that-will-inspire-you.html

https://en.wikipedia.org/wiki/LeBron_James

https://www.brainyquote.com/authors/lebron-james-quotes

https://www.brainyquote.com/authors/lebron-james-quotes

https://www.lebronjames.com/

Made in United States
Troutdale, OR
09/21/2023

13090349R00042